AN ALPHABET OF
GARDEN FLOWERS

AN

ALPHABET

OF

GARDEN FLOWERS

MARIE ANGEL

PELHAM BOOKS

First published in Great Britain by
Pelham Books Ltd
27 Wrights Lane
London W8 5TZ
1987

British Library Cataloguing in Publication Data

Angel, Marie
An alphabet of garden flowers.
1. Angiosperms——Dictionaries
I. Title
582.13′03′21   QK495.A1

ISBN 0-7207-1775-2

Typeset by Goodfellow and Egan Ltd, Cambridge
Printed and bound in Italy by
Arnoldo Mondadori, Verona

FOR
MY MOTHER AND FATHER

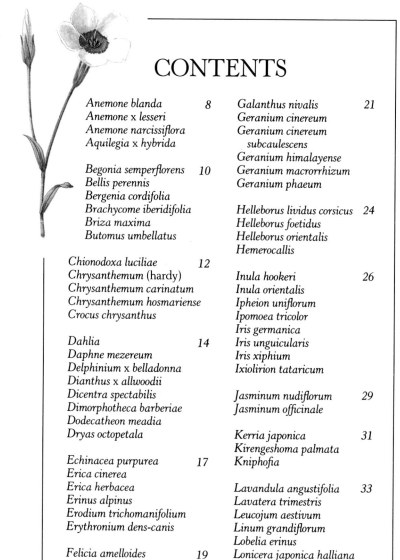

CONTENTS

Anemone blanda: From a handful of unpromising, small, black, wrinkled tubers, planted in autumn, *A. blanda* will enrich the garden with a sheet of intensely blue, starry flowers in February and March. The tripartite leaves enfold a single, many-rayed flower, which remains closed on dull days but opens responsively to the sun. The variety 'White Splendour' has an equally beautiful flower with glistening white petals rather larger than the species. Anemones should be planted where they receive sunshine in the spring, but are shaded during the summer. If left undisturbed, they will increase quite quickly.

Anemone x *lesseri*: a garden hybrid from A. *multifida* x *A. sylvestris*, in early summer the rich, rose-pink flowers shine above the clumps of five-lobed leaves of deep, glossy, green.

Anemone narcissiflora: this is a taller plant suited to a wild garden. From May to July leafy umbels of white flowers, with green centres surrounded with golden stamens, rise from tufts of deeply-cut, lobed leaves. The buds are sometimes flushed with a soft pinky-purple.

Aquilegia x *hybrida*: the flowers of the long-spurred cultivar are borne on tall stems above pale green, ferny foliage. The hybrids are bred in many colours – pink, red, crimson, blue, yellow, cream and white.

1 *Anemone blanda* 'White Splendour'
2 *Anemone blanda* 3 *Anemone* x *lesseri*
4 *Anemone narcissiflora* ABOVE *Aquilegia* x *hybrida*

Begonia semperflorens 'Treasure Trove': a fibrous-rooted begonia much used for summer bedding, or in tubs and window-boxes, it flowers continuously from early summer until the first frosts. A few plants potted up and brought into the house in autumn will stay in bloom all winter. Some cultivars have bronze or purple leaves. This particular variety has pretty bicolour flowers with sea-shell petals.

Bellis perennis 'Dresden China': this is a miniature double daisy with tightly quilled petals and a demure, prim appearance. Its neat habit and prolific flowering makes it ideal for a window-box, the front of the border or for edging a cottage-garden path. Other varieties of these button-shaped daisies come in shades of red, rose and white.

Bergenia cordifolia: a member of the saxifrage family, it has big, evergreen, leathery leaves, which become tinged with red and purple in winter. In early spring the flowerheads begin to appear deep among the leaves, but the thick stalks of mauve-pink, bell-shaped flowers do not rise above them until warmer days arrive. Bergenias will grow virtually anywhere and are often used as ground-cover. There are a number of named varieties to be had in different pinks, red and white.

Brachycome iberidifolia (Swan River Daisy): this charming half-hardy annual from Australia is easily grown from a packet of seeds. The long succession of daisy-like flowers in lavender blue, white and pink stars the mounds of ferny foliage.

Briza maxima (Great Quaking Grass): an annual grass, it has panicles of drooping, ovoid spikelets shimmering silvery-green and tinged with purple; its narrow leaves grow in tufts.

Butomus umbellatus: a rush-like, aquatic perennial with tall, linear leaves triangular in section, its umbels of pink flowers rise on tall stems in summer and early autumn. This is a fine plant to grow in a boggy place or in shallow water at the edge of a pond or lake.

1 *Begonia semperflorens* 'Treasure Trove'
2 *Butomus umbellatus* 3 *Bergenia cordifolia*
4 *Briza maxima* 5 *Bellis perennis* 'Dresden China' ABOVE *Brachycome iberidifolia*

11

Chionodoxa luciliae (Glory of the Snow): a small, bulbous plant, it quickly spreads itself if left undisturbed. The charming, soft-blue flowers with white centres bloom in March. It does well in ordinary garden soil in a sunny spot.

Chrysanthemum (hardy garden): there are literally hundreds of varieties of early-flowering chrysanthemums, which came originally from the wild Chinese and Japanese species, to grow out-of-doors in the mixed border or for cut flowers. Buds may be pinched off to give larger blooms, but modern varieties such as Korean, spray, pom-pom and rubellum are intended to be grown as sprays. The flowers, which may be single or double, come in rich crimsons and reds, bronze and gold as well as subtler shades of pinks, primrose and white.

Chrysanthemum carinatum: this very colourful, annual chrysanthemum has bright green leaves, deeply lobed. The large, single flowers are carried on stiff, erect stems; the central disc is dark and the ray-florets are banded with various colours, like a target, or a bright parasol.

Chrysanthemum hosmariense: a hardy plant, it makes a sprawling mat of grey-green leaves and is covered during the summer months with typical daisy flowers of glistening white with deep golden discs.

Crocus chrysanthus 'Cream Beauty': this early-flowering form of crocus brightens the dark days of February. The warm, cream colour of the petals and the golden throat are accentuated by the vermilion stigmas. It naturalises well in grass.

1 *Chrysanthemum* (hardy varieties)
2 *Chrysanthemum hosmariense*
3 *Chrysanthemum carinatum* ABOVE
Chionodoxa luciliae and *Crocus Chrysanthus*
'Cream Beauty'

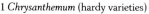

Dahlia: there are many varieties of dahlia and they are deservedly popular. The Collerette dahlias (Class III) have a single outer ring of ray-florets and an inner ring of small florets, with the centre forming a disc. They are very attractive and may be had in a large number of colour variations – the crisp ruff of central petals usually paler than the outer ones.

Daphne mezereum: this is a deciduous shrub that grows into a low bush. The small, heavily scented flowers wreath the naked stems in winter and early spring. It should be planted close to the house, or on a frequently used path, so that the delicious fragrance and charming colour may be often enjoyed, even during inclement weather. Daphnes have an inexplicable way of dying off, so cuttings should be propagated every year or plants raised from seed.

Delphinium x *belladonna* 'Cliveden Beauty': the belladonna delphiniums have a lightness and charm not given to the giant border varieties. The single flowers are well spaced out on the stems so that a group in the border has the airy flutter of a cloud of blue butterflies.

Dianthus x *allwoodii* 'Doris': the 'allwoodii' pinks are the result of crosses between perpetual flowering carnations and old-fashioned garden pinks. 'Doris' forms strong rosettes of silvery-blue leaves, and gives a long succession of flowers of good substance, the petals a delicate salmon-pink with a deeper central zone. A well-drained soil with the addition of some lime, and a place in full sunshine suits most Dianthus. Pinks make good edgings for borders, or for underplanting in rose-beds.

Dicentra spectabilis (Bleeding Heart): a beautiful plant from Japan, its handsome, deeply-cut, glaucous leaves make a perfect foil for the rosy-crimson, heart-shaped flowers that dangle from tall, arching stems, like a row of Victorian lockets.

Dimorphotheca barberiae: a perennial from South Africa with downy aromatic leaves, it must be placed in full sunshine, as the rayed daisy flowers do not open in the shade or on dull days.

1 *Dahlia Collerette* (Class III) 2 *Delphinium* x *belladonna* 'Cliveden Beauty' 3 *Dianthus* x *allwoodii* 'Doris' 4 *Dicentra spectabilis* 5 *Daphne mezereum* 6 *Dryas octopetala* ABOVE *Dimorphotheca barberiae* FOLLOWING PAGE *Dodecatheon meadia*

Dodecatheon meadia (Shooting Stars): from a tuft of long, blunt leaves, erect stems carry the umbels of rich pink cyclamen-like flowers, which give a firework display in late spring. Dodecatheons need to be grown in a moisture-retentive soil, in sun or light shade.

Dryas octopetala (Mountain Avens): a native of scree and rocks of the high mountains of Europe and the Arctic, its leathery leaves are dark green above and felted, greyish-white below. The flowers usually, but not always, have eight petals, hence the name – octopetala – or eight-petalled. When the white flowers are over, the fruits develop delightful, fluffy heads similar to those of clematis or pulsatillas.

1 *Erica herbacea* 'King George' 2 *Erodium trichomanifolium* 3 *Erinus alpinus* 4 *Erythronium dens-canis* 5 *Erica cinerea* 'Purple Beauty' PAGE 18 *Echinacea purpurea*

Echinacea purpurea: a hardy, herbaceous perennial from North America, it is a tall plant suitable for a sunny border. The leaves are slightly toothed and rough to the touch and the large, rosy-crimson flowers have dark, conical centres.

Erica cinerea and *E. herbacea*: ericas are hardy evergreens which make good groundcover. They need an open situation in full sun. Most heathers prefer peaty soils, but *E. herbacea* is tolerant of lime and therefore useful on chalky soils. The variety 'King George' has narrow bells of deep rose-pink which start to appear in autumn and continue through until spring. *E. cinerea* 'Purple Beauty', with its deep green linear leaves and racemes of large bell-shaped flowers of rich purple-carmine, provides colour during summer and autumn.

Erinus alpinus: this is a hardy perennial with dark green spathulate leaves forming a good tuft. Flowerheads will appear as early as March and continue through the year. The upright stems of bright-pink flowers almost cover the plant when it is at the height of its flowering. Any well-drained garden soil will suit this alpine; it will grow in a crevice in the rock garden or on a drystone wall.

Erodium trichomanifolium: this plant has pale-grey leaves rather like silver parsley; wiry stems hold sprays of white flowers with maroon and crimson pencillings. It needs a well-drained, sunny spot in a trough or rock garden.

Erythronium dens-canis (Dog's-tooth Violet): this has very handsome foliage, mottled and blotched with maroon. The flowers come singly to a stem in April and May, with deep, pinky-mauve reflexed petals, paling to white in the centre, which is gold. It is variable in colour, and there are a number of named varieties available. Grow in humus-rich, moist soil under shrubs or deciduous trees where they are shaded during the summer months and leave undisturbed.

Felicia amelloides (Blue Marguerite): a bushy, half-hardy perennial from South Africa, it is often grown as an annual, as it will only come through the winter in milder areas. The leaves are ovate and a fresh green. The sky-blue daisies on tall stems have a bright yellow eye and bloom from June to August – and even later in mild places. It needs a well-drained soil and a sunny sheltered position.

1 *Felicia pappei* 2 *Felicia amelloides* 3 *Fuchsia magellanica molinae* 4 *Fuchsia* 'Golden Marinka' 5 *Fuchsia* 'Coachman' FOLLOWING PAGE *Freesia* x *kewensis*

Felicia pappei: a perennial species with finely cut, almost succulent, leaves of a good light green, the lovely china-blue daisies appear in July and continue until the frosts. Both these Felicias are good in tubs and window-boxes.

Freesia x *kewensis* (garden hybrids): freesias are not really hardy except in frost-free areas, but specially prepared corms may now be bought, which if planted out-of-doors in April flower in July and August. There are many different colours available. Freesias may also be grown under glass.

Fuchsia magellanica molinae: a very hardy, erect, bushy plant, it will come through even severe winters unscathed. The leaves are a bright, light green and the slender, delicate flowers white turning to the palest shell-pink. It is best grown in not too rich a soil, in the sunniest location possible, where it will give the finest show.

Fuchsia 'Coachman': a rapid grower with stout stems, it is often trained into a standard. The leaves are pale green and the flowers hang in clusters. The calyx, which has an elongated tube, is a soft flamingo-pink, with the short, single corolla a deep salmon colour. Only half-hardy, this fuchsia is excellent in large containers or in the border during the summer.

Fuchsia 'Golden Marinka': this is a very striking fuchsia, useful for hanging baskets because of its trailing habit. The broad leaves are handsomely variegated above with yellow, the undersides being a deep magenta. The single flowers flash out against the flamboyant leaves, with bright red calyx and corolla of a deeper crimson, with a long tassel of shining red stamens.

Galanthus nivalis: the well-loved snowdrop braves the bitter cold of January and February, spreading its delicate winged petals over the receding snow. These bulbs should always be transplanted 'in the green', that is as soon as the flowers have faded.

Geranium cinereum 'Apple Blossom' and *G.c.* 'Laurence Flatman': as a family, geraniums have highly attractive rounded, palmate-lobed leaves, often deeply cut, and so decorative they are worth growing for their foliage alone.

1 *Geranium himalayense* 2 *G. cinereum* 'Laurence Flatman' 3 *G. phaeum* 4 *G. cinereum subcaulescens* 5 *G. macrorrhizum* Album 6 *G. cinereum* 'Apple Blossom' PAGE 23 *Galanthus nivalis*

The orbicular flowers come in a wide range of colours, from intense purple-blue through brilliant magenta, to soft pinks and white. 'Laurence Flatman' is a long-lived hybrid with seven-lobed, fretted, grey-green leaves, from which appear, over a long period, cupped flowers stained with deep pink, and heavily veined in crimson-purple, with a dark eye ornamented with dusky stamens and anthers; it is a sun-lover, suitable for the front of the border or the rock garden. Most geraniums have veined petals, and in some varieties, such as 'Laurence Flatman', this is a remarkable feature. 'Apple Blossom', a vigorous, free-flowering hybrid, makes small mounds of silvery-green leaves from which come a succession of flowers of palest pink, the petals lightly veined. This plant needs a sunny position in the trough or rock garden.

Geranium cinereum subcaulescens: this is a low-growing plant with rounded, greyish leaves, from which rise sprays of brilliant cerise flowers with a black centre. Needing a sunny position in a well-drained soil, it flowers from June to August.

Geranium himalayense (syn. G. *meeboldii*, G. *grandiflorum*): the lobed leaves of this plant are deeply cleft and toothed, with distinctive veining. The bowl-shaped flowers are a rich blue with a hint of violet; their crimson veins are very apparent when the sun shines through the silky petals. A rhizomatous plant from Sikkim, it flowers in early summer; it may be propagated by division in spring and autumn, or by seed in spring.

Geranium macrorrhizum Album: this has five-lobed leaves, which when crushed are strongly aromatic. The charming flowers have a very rounded calyx which is flushed with red, as are the stems and leaves. From the South Eastern Alps and Balkans, it has a spreading growth that makes ideal groundcover. It will grow just about anywhere and may be divided up in spring or autumn.

Geranium phaeum (the 'Mourning Widow'): a native of Great Britain, it is becoming increasingly rare in the wild. A tallish plant, with deeply lobed and notched leaves, the flowers are very dark, looking almost black, of a deep crimson-maroon, each petal crimped as if with a goffering iron. In happy conditions this attractive plant soon colonises itself, and will do so in damp shade or under hedges.

ELLEBORES

Helleborus lividus corsicus: hellebores are useful perennials, some flowering during the winter months. They require a semi-shaded situation, where the soil is well-drained but not dry. The flower heads remain as a decorative feature well into summer. *H. l. corsicus* thrusts up robust, fingered foliage of a lightish green, the curved leaves edged with small spines. The clustered flowerheads of pale apple-green appear very early in the year, the rounded petals forming shallow cups filled with a mass of creamy stamens.

Helleborus foetidus: this hellebore has dark green, narrowly divided leaves with saw edges. The leaves make a large clump when established, providing the perfect background for the light-green flower stems and buds, which appear as early as November; the nodding, bell-shaped flowers have petals delicately edged with crimson.

Helleborus orientalis: is a very variable plant, the upright, slightly branched, flower-heads surmount the broad, divided leaves in March and April. The flowers are often freckled or heavily dappled within; they can be white, pink, or deep purple-pink, and some so deeply coloured as to be almost black. The purply-pink and other deeper colours appear to have a soft bloom on the outer petals. The flowers nod, and must be tipped upwards to appreciate the charm of their interiors.

Hemerocallis x hybrid cultivar (Day Lily): these useful, perennial plants soon make large patches of broad strap-like leaves, which when they break through the ground very early in the year are a pale, yellow-green darkening later. The lily-like flowers are borne on tall stems, and a long period of flowering may be obtained by planting early, intermediate and late varieties.

1 *Helleborus orientalis* 2 *H. foetidus* 3 *H. lividus corsicus* ABOVE *Hemerocallis* x hybrid cultivar

Inula hookeri and *Inula orientalis*: inulas are good, hardy, herbaceous perennials and make large clumps in the border in a moisture-retentive soil. The bushy plants are surmounted in the summer by big daisy-like heads. *Inula orientalis* has large raised discs, with thread-like, slightly drooping ray-florets in a golden yellow. *Inula hookeri* has flowers with a flatter disc and longer, slender petals in a clear yellow.

Ipheion uniflorum 'Wisley Blue': this bulb from South America spreads quickly by offsets, sending up tufts of long, thin leaves, which smell of onions if crushed. The tubular, starry flowers are solitary on long stems, a pale milky-blue in the type but a deeper, mauvy-blue in the

'Wisley Blue' variety. Each sepal has a definite dark medial line, which adds to the star face of the blossom.

Ipomoea tricolor 'Heavenly Blue' (Morning Glory): a half-hardy climbing plant similar to the wild convolvulus, it needs a hot summer to give a fine display if grown out-of-doors; in a conservatory or greenhouse, it gives a glorious show from August through September. Each morning, from among the heart-shaped leaves, the long, elegant buds unfurl to reveal stupendous trumpets of pure sky-blue silk. By early evening these ephemeral flowers are fading and crumpling to limp rags – Cinderellas of a day. Dead-heading will ensure a continuous succession of flowers. The seed should be soaked in warm water for twenty-four hours before sowing; as they dislike being transplanted, sow straight into peat pots, which can be planted out without up-setting the roots. The seeds germinate well with gentle bottom heat, in propagators or a greenhouse.

Iris germanica hybrid (bearded iris): a rhizomatous iris, the sword-shaped blue-green leaves grow in fans from the rhizome. The large spectacular flowers on tall stems appear from late May to June, according to the variety. The upper petals, known as standards, are ruffled and curve inwards; the lower petals, or falls, flare out crisply beneath them. In some varieties the falls are velvety in texture, in others veined or striated with colour. Some plants have scented flowers.

1 *Iris xiphium* hybrid 'Exotic Beauty' 2 *Iris germanica* hybrid 3 *Inula orientalis* 4 *Inula hookeri* 5 *Ipomoea tricolor* 'Heavenly Blue' 6 *Ipheion uniflorum* 'Wisley Blue' 7 *Ixiolirion tataricum* FOLLOWING PAGE *Iris unguicularis*

Iris unguicularis (*I. stylosa*): a winter-flowering iris from Algeria, it should be planted in a well-drained, sunny position, preferably against a south-facing wall. The plants take time to settle down before the soft lavender-blue flowers appear among the grassy leaves, surprising the dark winter days with their fragile, shimmering loveliness. Picked in furled bud and brought into a warm room, the petals unfold visibly and a delicate scent is released. Sometimes flowering starts as early as October and continues through until March.

Iris xiphium cultivars: a bulbous iris of stiff upright growth, it needs a well-drained soil and a sunny position. The bulbs flower early in June, and come in a good colour range – white, yellow, bronze, blue and purple – and mixtures of these colours.

Ixiolirion tataricum: this is a bulbous plant with tufted, grass-like leaves. In early summer the flower stems appear with umbels of purple-blue bells. Not very hardy, it should be planted in a warm, sheltered spot, and protected from frost.

Jasminum nudiflorum and *J. officinale*: the common jasmines are hardy plants, although a hard winter will cut back young, tender growth of *J. officinale*. *J. officinale* flowers in summer, while *J. nudiflorum* provides much needed colour.

1 *Jasminum nudiflorum* 2 *J. officinale*

for the winter months. An almost ever-green climber, with beautiful dark-green, pinnate leaves, *J. officinale* grows best in a sheltered situation. A rampant climber, it will quickly cover porches, arbours or south-facing walls. Plant it where its penetrating fragrance may be appreciated on the warm evening air, and its tubular white flowers will glimmer through the dusk like stars against a mass of intricate foliage. *J. nudiflorum* is a deciduous shrub that will climb if trained on a support. When the trifoliate leaves drop in autumn, brilliant, pure yellow, trumpet-shaped flowers are borne on the leafless stems, a cheering sight during the winter. It flowers more prolifically when planted in a sunny spot, but will accept a less favourable site with equanimity.

1 *Kerria japonica* Pleniflora 2 *Kniphofia* hybrid 'Bee's Lemon' 3 *Kniphofia* hybrid 'Royal Standard' 4 *Kniphofia* hybrid 'Bee's Sunset' 5 *Kirengeshoma palmata*

Kerria japonica Pleniflora: a trouble-free deciduous shrub from China, it flowers in early spring, the green canes putting on their leaves and flowers almost simultaneously. The double variety has many-petalled, orange-yellow pom-poms all along the branches in a riotous display, matching well the daffodils, narcissi and primroses in flower at the same time.

Kirengeshoma palmata (Waxbells): this herbaceous woodland plant from Japan requires moist soil and partial shade. The leaves are rounded, lobed and slightly hairy. The flower buds, which may be seen from early summer, do not reveal their beauty until the drooping, creamy-yellow, waxy flower bells open in September.

Kniphofia (Red-hot Poker, Torch Lily): *K.* 'Bee's Sunset', *K.* 'Bee's Lemon', and *K.* 'Royal Standard' are all hybrids excellent in the mixed border or used in a group as a focal point. The glaucus-green, narrow, rush-like leaves make large clumps from which rise during the summer stout leafless stems bearing the many tubular flowers in poker-like formation. Among the many garden hybrids there is a good colour range, from creamy-white to the fiercest red, with flowering periods varying from June to October.

1 *Lonicera japonica halliana* 2 *Leucojum aestivum* 3 *Lavatera trimestris* 4 *Lavandula angustifolia* 5 *Lobelia erinus* 'Crystal Palace' (dark blue) 6 *Lobelia erinus* 'Red Cascade' (pink) 7 *Lobelia erinus* 'Cambridge Blue' (light blue) PAGE 34 *Linum grandiflorum* 'Bright Eyes'

Lavandula angustifolia: this is the old-fashioned lavender, an evergreen shrub from the Mediterranean. Sometimes used as a low hedge in herb gardens, or to edge a path, the whole plant is fragrant if brushed against. The bushes are densely covered with silver-grey, linear leaves and in late summer the flower-heads, on long erect stalks, open their tubular mauve flowers. The sweetly-scented spikes always attract an attendant swarm of bees and butterflies.

Lavatera trimestris (Silver Cup): a showy annual also from the Mediterranean area, it is very easily grown from seed.

The leaves are roundish and pale green. The large trumpet flowers are a clear silvery-pink, with a silky sheen. There are deeper pinks available, and a beautiful, glacial white form.

Leucojum aestivum (Summer Snowflake): this bulbous perennial plant is easy to grow in ordinary garden soil, in a lightly shaded and, preferably, damp position. Flowering in late spring rather than summer, the bulb throws up a lot of bright-green, shining, strap-like leaves; from a green spathe at the top of the erect stems hang several, white, belled flowers, each petal tipped with a green spot, somewhat similar to a snowdrop. Now an uncommon, localised, native plant, it is widespread in Europe and Asia Minor.

Linum grandiflorum 'Bright Eyes': a hardy annual to grow from seed scattered where required, this variety is particularly charming. Another form is the well-known 'Rubrum', which has crimson petals.

Lobelia erinus: this half-hardy perennial is usually grown as an annual. The following are all garden cultivars to grow from seed, but they are commonly bought as small plants from nurseries in early summer: *L. e.* 'Crystal Palace' is a compact grower with bronzy foliage and deep rich blue flowers; *L. e.* 'Cambridge Blue' is similar in habit, but with green leaves and light blue flowers; *L. e.* 'Red Cascade' is a trailing variety for use in hanging baskets, containers or window-boxes. The flowers are magenta-pink, with a white eye.

Lonicera japonica halliana: a rampant climber, this ever-green honeysuckle will quickly cover a fence or pillar or run over a hedge, but it is easy to trim with shears to keep it in bounds. The paired, tubular flowers are white at first, but age to a warm gold; they are intensely fragrant and appear all summer long.

Matricaria eximia (Feverfew): a perennial plant grown as a herb for many centuries, it has pretty oak-like leaves and heads of white daisy-flowers with yellow discs. It will seed itself round the garden once it is established, and stays green all the year round.

Meconopsis cambrica: the Welsh poppy is a native plant with deeply cut, hairy leaves and flowers of sharp, cool yellow or orange. It will colonise itself, and can be invasive, but is ideal for wilder corners of the garden. Deadheading the bottle-shaped seed-heads will help to prevent seedlings, and also prolong the flowering season.

Mentha suaveolens Variegata (Pineapple mint): mints are very easy to grow, provided that the soil is retentive of

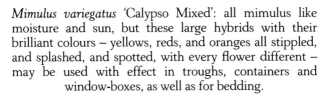

moisture. The flowers of this mint
are not conspicuous in colour; it is
grown more for its very decorative
leaves and its scent.

Mimulus cupreus 'Highland Red': a dwarf plant
for a moist situation, this mimulus has masses
of brilliant red flowers and would do well in full
sun in the bog garden, or at the edge of a pond.

Mimulus variegatus 'Calypso Mixed': all mimulus like
moisture and sun, but these large hybrids with their
brilliant colours – yellows, reds, and oranges all stippled,
and splashed, and spotted, with every flower different –
may be used with effect in troughs, containers and
window-boxes, as well as for bedding.

Mirabilis jalapa (Marvel of Peru): a plant from tropical
America, it is usually grown as an annual. The fragrant
trumpet-shaped flowers can be yellow, pink, crimson and
white; they open half-way through the afternoon and fade
away the next morning. In dull or cool weather they stay
open longer.

Myosotis sylvatica 'Blue Ball': forget-me-nots grow so
easily from seed that once plants are in the garden they
sow themselves, with seedlings coming up everywhere.
However, the self-sown flowers eventually pale to a
wishy-washy colour, so it is worthwhile to sow seeds of
good blue varieties such as 'Blue Ball', which makes
rounded, compact plants, with sprays of bright blue
flowers.

1 *Myosotis sylvatica* 'Blue Ball' 2 *Mentha
suaveolens* Variegata (variegated leaves)
3 *Matricaria eximia* 4 *Meconopsis cambrica*
5 *Mimulus cupreus* 'Highland Red' 6 *Mimulus
variegatus* 'Calypso Mixed' ABOVE *Mirabilis
jalapa*

Narcissus cyclamineus 'Jenny': a dainty, early-flowering narcissus, with pale, swept-back petals, like wings, and a light-yellow cup. Less than a foot in height, they look well in containers of any sort, in the wild garden, or on an alpine lawn.

Narcissus triandrus Albus (Angel's Tears): this is a fragile beauty, a few inches high, for the rock garden, window-box or trough, where the charming, nodding heads and reflexed petals do not have to compete with larger plants.

Nemophila menziesii (Baby Blue Eyes): a hardy annual of spreading habit, with deeply-cut leaves, the vivid blue, bowl-shaped flowers have a conspicuous white centre, and are carried in profusion from June to August.

Nicotiana alata 'Lime Green': this half-hardy perennial has sticky leaves and buds. The long tubular flowers have soft yellow-green petals, which, like a lot of greenish flowers, are very popular with flower arrangers. They need a good, rich soil and a sunny site for the best results.

Nigella damascena (Love-in-a-mist): an erect, bushy, hardy annual, with finely cut leaves, it has butterfly-blue flowers veiled with filmy green ruffs. The large seedheads are valued for their decorative quality.

Nymphaea pygmaea Alba: the smallest of all waterlilies, it has the typical leaves and flower shape of the larger species, but with all the added charm of the perfect miniature. It is small enough to grow happily in a container, such as a tub, or a tiny pool, providing that it catches the sun. It will grow successfully in less than a foot of water – ideal for a lead cistern in the restricted space of a town garden.

1 *Narcissus cyclamineus* 'Jenny' 2 *Narcissus triandrus* Albus 3 *Nigella damascena*
4 *Nicotiana alata* 'Lime Green' 5 *Nemophila menziesii* ABOVE *Nymphaea pygmaea* Alba

Oenothera missouriensis: this trailing evening primrose covers a lot of ground with its stems and leaves. From June onwards the buds – usually spotted with red – open to reveal large, crumpled petals of coolest lemon. Like most oenothera the flowers open at dusk, but stay on the plant for several days.

Olearia macrodonta: a large hardy shrub from New Zealand, the leaves are somewhat like those of the holly, but the undersides are felted with white. In summer the bush is covered with clusters of small, white, daisy-flowers.

Omphalodes cappadocica: this hardy perennial forms slow-spreading clumps by means of creeping rhizomes. The light green leaves on long stalks are hairy above. In May the sprays of gentian-blue flowers begin to appear among the foliage. Give this plant semi-shade and a moist soil for preference.

Ornithogalum nutans: a hardy bulb that will quickly naturalize in the right conditions, it is useful for the wilder corners of the garden, and under shrubs, as it thrives in light shade. The flowers appear in April and May, its erect stems bearing spikes of green and white striped bells.

Oxalis adenophylla: a beautiful species from Chile, *Oxalis adenophylla* has a small bulb-like rhizome, covered with coarse fibres. The glaucous, drooping, clover-like leaves die down in the winter, resurrecting themselves each spring to frame the exquisite buds, furled as tightly as a parasol, and opening to silver-pink petals veined with deeper carmine, with a dark eye in the centre. This tiny plant likes full sunshine – its flowers fail to open on a dull day.

Oxalis corniculata (Sleeping Beauty): this small plant seeds itself around the garden. It has loose heads of bright yellow flowers, and the clover-like leaves fold downwards at night, hence the country name.

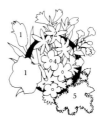

1 *Oenothera missouriensis* 2 *Ornithogalum nutans* 3 *Omphalodes cappadocica* 4 *Oxalis adenophylla* 5 Olearia macrodonta ABOVE *Oxalis corniculata*

41

Primula auricula (Bear's Ears): an alpine plant that needs good drainage but is otherwise easy to grow. The thick, ear-shaped leaves are often edged and generously covered with meal, which will rub off if handled. The stout stems hold up whorls of velvety flowers in jewel colours, with a white centre and a rich fragrance. Alpine, or Border auriculas, are not damaged by cold weather, but the more specialist Show auriculas need the protection of glass, either in a cool greenhouse, or an indoor windowsill to keep them in perfect condition.

Primula capitata: this summer flowering primula will tolerate dryish conditions. The leaves have a thick coating of meal, as have also the stem and flowerhead, which consists of many buds clustered together. Against this powdery background the petals unfold their imperial purple.

Primula marginata: an alpine primula that has rosettes of spoon-shaped leaves with a decorative deckle edge lined with meal. The umbels of lilac-coloured flowers delight the eye in April and May. It does well tucked into a crevice in the rock garden, preferring light shade and a well-drained soil with a little lime.

Primula rosea: a moisture-loving primula happiest planted in drifts in a bog-garden, the rounded buds of intense carmine-pink thrust their way through the soil in early spring before the leaves. As the stem lengthens the several flowers unfold and the leaves begin to appear, bronzy at first, gradually turning to green.

Primula sieboldii: this woodland primula from Japan likes a loamy soil and damp shade. The delightful crinkly leaves appear year after year in spring together with the flowers. There are many named cultivars, and the largish flowers may be had in a range of white, pink, magenta, lilac blue and white, stippled or veined with colour; the petals may be fringed and ruffled, or cut to give the appearance of a snowflake.

1 *Primula marginata* 2 *P. capitata* 3 *P. sieboldii* 4 *P. auricula* 5 *P. rosea* 6 *P.* x *tommasinii* (garden hybrid) ABOVE *Pulsatilla vulgaris*

The whole plant is light and graceful, suitable for planting under deciduous trees, receiving spring sunshine, but being shaded from it later in the year.

Primula x *tommasinii*(Polyanthus): a hybrid of garden origin that is popular as a border or bedding plant, also in window-boxes and tubs, or as a houseplant. Modern strains have provided a very wide range of colours: white and pale yellows, rich golds, ambers, apricots and tawnies, palest pink to rich Tyrian velvets, scarlets and ruby crimsons, golden browns, and many shades of blue. All these colours are further enriched with the shape and colour of the distinctive starry eye which embellishes each flower.

Pulsatilla vulgaris (Pasque Flower): a well-established plant makes a round clump of silky-haired, finely divided leaves. In spring, the flowers appear before the leaves have fully developed. The petals are covered on the outside, like the leaves, with fine silky hairs; inside, the colour varies from deep purple to pale lilac, with a large boss of golden stamens. The seedheads mature into soft feathery balls that are very decorative. A native of calcareous downland, the Pasque Flower prefers lime but will grow in any fertile soil with an open sunny situation.

Quamoclit coccinea: a half-hardy annual from south-eastern United States of America, it will grow to nine feet under the right conditions. It would need a very sheltered position out of doors, but revels in the protection of a conservatory or greenhouse. *Quamoclit coccinea* has large, rich green, heart-shaped leaves and the flowers, long narrow trumpets, scarlet with golden throats, grow in small clusters, exotically brilliant among the foliage.

Seeds should be sown under glass in gentle heat. It helps germination to soak them in warm water for twenty-four hours before placing them two or three to a pot. It is important that the roots are not damaged when transplanting.

Quamoclit pennata (Cypress Vine): another similar vine from tropical America, with very finely cut and divided leaves that are decorative in themselves. The scarlet, funnel-shaped flowers curve like claws and grow in racemes from the axils of the leaves.

1 *Rosa* 'Fantin-Latour' 2 *R.* 'Boule de Neige' 3 *R.* 'Koenigin von Danemarck' 4 *R.* 'Madame Pierre Oger' 5 *R.* 'Stanwell Perpetual' PAGE 48 *R.* 'Complicata'

Rosa 'Boule de Neige' (Bourbon 1867): a tallish rose with glossy green leaves, the buds are marked with crimson, but open to reveal creamy-white petals, forming an almost globular, fragrant bloom. It flowers in summer and again in the autumn.

R. 'Complicata' (shrub/climber): the very large single blooms have petals of brilliant pink, lighter towards the centre, with showy, golden stamens. The flowers appear all along the tall, arching stems, which may be six or seven feet in length. This rose grows easily to at least eight feet high and as much wide – but if space is available, it is worth a place for its dazzling display in June. Probably a hybrid of *R. macrantha* it originated in Europe some time this century.

R. 'Fantin-Latour' (centifolia hybrid *c.* 1900): from a rounded bud, the petals unfold to form a cupped flower of many fluted and pleated petals in a delicious pale-pink, deepening in the centre. This delicately scented rose is a strong grower with large, smooth leaves. A lovely rose of unknown origin, it is named after the French painter, who so ably portrayed this type of rose.

R. 'Koenigin von Danemarck' (alba 1826): this is a rose with superb blooms, fully quartered, and packed with many folded and crimped pink petals, deeper towards the centre and gathered into a green button eye. This richly scented rose grows into an elegant bush, with the bluish-green foliage of the albas.

R. 'Madame Pierre Oger' (Bourbon shrub 1878): a sport from 'La Reine Victoria', it is similar in size and shape, with deeply cupped, sweetly scented flowers, the petals of palest blush-pink, with a touch of carmine on the buds and edges of the petals.

R. 'Stanwell Perpetual' (shrub 1838): this shrub rose throws up arching branches of small ferny foliage. The flattish, semi-double flowers are a soft-pink, fading to white, and deliciously fragrant. This rose blooms all the summer and well into the autumn – hence its name.

Salpiglossis sinuata 'Grandiflora': a decorative plant to grow from seed, and to use in a mixed border or in pots. The voluptuous trumpet flowers have a rich, velvety texture, and come in many jewel colours, the petals veined and netted in darker or contrasting colours. The leaves are linear, wavy at the edges and rather sparse.

These plants need the support of twiggy sticks or canes.

1 *Salpiglossis sinuata* 'Grandiflora'
2 *Sarcococca confusa* 3 *Symphytum caucasicum* 4 *Saxifraga* x *boydii* 5 *Saxifraga* x *Jenkinsae* 6 *Scabiosa caucasia* 'Clive Greaves' 7 *Sisyrinchium bermudiana* PAGE 51 *Senecio laxifolius*

Sarcococca confusa: not only a good evergreen plant for groundcover, with a dense and spreading habit, the small, creamy flowers appearing in the axils of the leaves during the winter months are also very fragrant, scenting the air for yards around. The flowers are followed by jet-black berries.

Saxifraga x *boydii* and *Saxifraga* x *Jenkinsae*: two little cushion-forming plants for a north-facing site in the rock garden – or preferably in a raised trough, where their miniature beauty may be seen more easily. The buds begin to peer through the tight leaf rosettes in early spring; at first they seem almost stemless, but grow taller as they mature.

Scabiosa caucasia 'Clive Greaves': this perennial border plant is excellent for cutting. The glaucous, divided leaves grow in a low compact mound. The large, lavender-blue flowers have a diaphanous, chiffon-and-tulle appearance. The lightest breeze stirs the heads, and they sway on their long, slender stems, like frothy Ascot hats. Scabious like sun and a dry position in well-drained soil.

Senecio laxifolius: a large spreading evergreen shrub, its oval leaves are margined with silver and felted white underneath; the young shoots and flowerbuds are also whitish. The sprays of small flowers are a bright sharp yellow against the grey and silver leaves. It is not entirely hardy – it may be cut back in severe winters.

Sisyrinchium bermudiana: reasonably hardy except in severe winters, its iris-like leaves grow in clumps, and the branched stems bear spathes from which come a succession of purple-blue, star-shaped flowers, with a yellow eye. Each flower only lives for a day, but several usually bloom at the same time on each stem.

Symphytum caucasicum: a good plant for the wild garden or damp, shady borders, its leaves are rough to the touch, and the plant is covered with tiny hairs on the foliage generally. The lobed, tubular flowers, produced in drooping sprays, are pinkish-red in bud and change to sky-blue as the flower matures.

Tagetes patula: this half-hardy annual from Mexico, is easily grown from seed and invaluable for the front of the border, edging, window boxes or containers, where it will flourish throughout the summer, impervious to weather conditions until cut down by the first frosts. These brilliant little flowers will grow even in poor soil, but prefer an open site in full sun. There are many garden varieties available in double and single form, all in gaudy, rich colours such as crimson petals with gold reverse, golden-yellow petals with scarlet blotch, deep mahogany splashed with gold, red blotched yellow, and plain reds and yellows. The dark green ferny leaves have a pungent smell if touched or crushed.

Thunbergia alata (Black-eyed Susan): an annual, self-clinging climber that will grow rapidly in the greenhouse or in a warm sheltered position in the garden. The flowers are freely produced and are an exotic apricot-orange with a sooty black eye. The seeds are often sold as a mixture, which includes soft yellows, cream, and white colours, some without the dark eye.

Tigridia pavonia (Peacock Tiger Flower): a half-hardy bulbous plant from South America, its narrow pleated leaves fan out in tufts. Long stems carry the triangular, ocelot-spotted flowers, which have three large, and three smaller petals, with the cupped centre heavily mottled with crimson. There are several named cultivars giving various reds, yellows, and white, but they are usually sold as a mixture.

Tradescantia virginiana (Trinity Flower, Spiderwort): this beautiful, hardy perennial plant is named in honour of John Tradescant, gardener to King Charles I. The leafy stems, up to two feet in height, have terminal umbels of silky, three-petalled flowers of intense blue-purple, embellished royally with orange-gold stamens. Most plants now grown in gardens are hybrids or selections from the original species. Colours are various shades of blue, from light to deep purple, and pure white with a blue centre. There is a long flowering period from June to September.

1 *Thunbergia alata* 2 *Tulipa tarda*
3 *Tradescantia virginiana* 4 *Tagetes patula*
5 *Tropaeolum peregrinum* ABOVE *Tigridia pavonia*

53

Tropaeolum peregrinum (Canary Creeper): a swift annual climber from Peru that can reach ten to twelve feet during the summer in a sunny sheltered position. The soft green, five-fingered leaves are a decorative background to the fringed yellow flowers, which smother the plant like a flight of jaunty, crested birds.

Tulipa tarda: short, curved leaves form a rosette, from which appear the short stems, each bearing several flowers. The petals, golden-yellow with a white tip on the inside and green and white on the outside, open wide and starry in the sun during early spring.

1 *Ursinia anethoides* 2 *Uvularia grandiflora*

Ursinia anethoides: a graceful plant with light-green feathery leaves, the large daisy flowers on long stems are orange with a dark zone round the central disc. There are garden varieties which are more compact in growth than the original species, and seed may be obtained in a mixture of orange and yellow shades. A half-hardy annual from South Africa, it must have a dry, sunny position for the best result, as the rayed flowers tend to fold up their petals during overcast conditions. Long periods of wet weather will also cause the plants to wilt and die. Ursinias make good pot plants if planted three or four to a six-inch pot.

Uvularia grandiflora (Bellwort, Merrybells): a rhizomatous, woodland plant from North America, it needs a moist, shady position in humus-rich soil. The branched stem has fragile, limp, perfoliate leaves, green above but with noticeably paler undersides. The drooping, soft-yellow flowers are bell-shaped, the petals tinged with green down the centre. The best time for planting Uvularias is from autumn to spring; the rhizomes may be lifted and divided during the same period.

1 *Verbena* x *hybrida* 2 *Viola* x *wittrockiana* 'Bambini Mixed' 3 *Viburnum farreri* 4 *Vinca major* 'Elegantissima' 5 *Viscaria oculata* PAGE 58 *Viola odorata* Alba

Verbena x *hybrida*: simple to grow from seed, *Verbena* will flourish cheerfully even in wet seasons. The plants have rounded heads of small, clustered flowers with the old-fashioned look of Victorian chintz. The colours of brilliant red, deep purple, mauves, pinks, and white are often set off with a distinctive white eye.

Viburnum farreri (*V. fragrans*): any plant that flowers profusely in winter, and is deliciously scented as well, is worth a special place in the garden. This deciduous viburnum bears small panicles of white flowers, pink in bud, from late autumn until spring, when the shrub is covered with the pinky-bronze of the early leaves.

Vinca major 'Elegantissima': undoubtedly one of the most decorative of the periwinkles, its leaves are blotched and bordered with cream. The plant grows in arching sprays, and for most of the year a few of the lilac-blue flowers may be found among the leaves. The graceful habit of the plant, and its ornamental leaves, lead to its use in flower arrangements. It is easily grown in shade, or partial shade.

Viola odorata Alba: the sweet violet, originally a wilding, but long cultivated in cottage gardens. The violet-tinged buds opening to white flowers are a welcome sight in early spring, as is their evanescent perfume.

Viola x *wittrockiana* 'Bambini Mixed': violas and pansies are another cottage garden plant, their velvety petals and subtle scent reminiscent of one's childhood delight in their whiskered faces, looking up like surprised kittens. 'Bambini' are particularly attractive, with prettily marked faces and vari-coloured petals.

Viscaria oculata: from a packet of seeds scattered in the front of the border, or between paving stones, comes a drift of confetti colours all through the summer, as the silky, round-eyed flowers stay until the first frosts.

Waldsteinia ternata: a good groundcover plant, whose natural habitat extends from Central Europe to Siberia and Japan, it will do well in a cool place. It makes clusters of trifoliate, deeply-incised leaves and has trailing woody stems; during the summer, it sends up sprays of cheerful, bright yellow blossoms, similar in shape to strawberry flowers.

1 *Weigela* Variegata 2 *Watsonia pyramidata* 3 *Waldsteinia ternata*

Watsonia pyramidata (Bugle Lily): this is a cormous perennial from South Africa, named after Sir William Watson, an eighteenth-century scientist. Every corm produces a fan-shaped sheaf of leaves similar to a gladiolus. From September until November the tall stems bear spikes of six-petalled, pinky-red flowers, each with a graceful curved tube. These plants require a sunny position and moisture during the growing period. Not fully hardy except in warmer areas, it needs the shelter of a frost-free greenhouse.

Weigela Variegata: an easy going shrub that will flourish in most gardens provided the soil is not too dry. This variety makes a compact bush, and the variegated leaves give a continual interest outside the flowering period. The clusters of bell-shaped flowers are pale-pink and come out in May and June, covering the whole bush.

Xeranthemum annuum (Immortelles): this well-known annual is grown not so much for its effect in the garden but for its quality as a dried flower. The erect stems and linear leaves are silver-grey, the leaves felted with white underneath. The solitary flowerheads are composed of bracts which look like daisy petals and are coloured in cerise-pink, mauve, white and purple. The centre florets are purple or white. Seed should be sown in April under glass or in May outside; the seedlings grow well in any normal soil. To dry the flowers, they should be cut just after they have fully opened, then made up into small bunches and hung up heads downward in a cool, airy place.

Yucca recurvifolia (Adam's Needle): this is a hardy variety, the one most often grown in English gardens, and is evergreen. It has a woody trunk which usually has to be about three feet high before a flowering stem appears. However, the long strap-like curved leaves, the lower ones arching downwards, are a feature in their own right. At intervals, usually in good hot summers, the yucca thrusts up branched stems of large, globular, belled flowers creamy-white in colour and with touches of crimson on the outer petals. Yuccas are used extensively in formal gardens and for growing in tubs and stone vases on terraces or as specimen plants on lawns. They do not need a rich soil and grow quite well in stony, poor soil, providing that it is well-drained.

Zantedeschia aethiopica: the South African arum lily, it grows in damp, marshy places. It is not reliably hardy except in frost-free areas, and is best grown in pots, outside in summer, indoors in winter. The variety 'Crowborough' is a much hardier plant, especially if deeply planted in moist soil, or below waterlevel, such as at the edge of a lake, or garden pool. It is always an extremely handsome plant, with broad

1 *Zantedeschia aethiopica* 2 *Zauschneria californica* 3 *Zinnia elegans* 4 *Zephyranthes grandiflora* 5 *Zigadenus elegans*

arrow-shaped leaves of shining malachite green. The tall, smooth stems are crowned by the large white spathe, which encircles and protects the golden spadix. Pot-grown plants should be dried off gradually after flowering and re-potted in fresh compost in October. Rhizomes and offsets may be divided and grown on separately at this time.

Zauschneria californica (California Fuchsia): A small, half-hardy perennial shrub, it needs a very sheltered, sun-baked corner, or it can be grown in a pot, and moved under cover for the winter. The stems of small, grey-green leaves weave a tangled mass, from which erupt the sprays of fiery vermilion trumpets in August to October.

Zephyranthes grandiflora: if grown in the open, this half-hardy bulb should be covered with a cloche, or given other protection during the winter, otherwise it is best grown in a pot under glass. The lovely rose-pink flowers appear among the grassy leaves late in the year. Potted plants should be left for some years without disturbance, as they appear to flower more freely when the bulbs become crowded in the pot. Any division or re-potting should be undertaken in the spring.

Zigadenus elegans (White Camass): a bulbous plant which forms itself into clumps, it has glaucous, linear leaves. During the summer, the quaint, greenish-white flowers appear in long racemes, with twinned, bright-green glands at the base of each petal, making a prominent ring round the stamens. This interesting plant needs a peaty, moist soil. Propagation is by seed, or division of the bulbs in autumn.

Zinnia elegans: another half-hardy plant which dislikes root disturbance, so seed is best sown in peat pots to facilitate transplanting. There are a great many cultivars now available for the garden, from large and tall to small and dwarf varieties. The oval, pointed leaves are a dull green and the upright, tough stems carry the solitary flowers above the foliage. The many-petalled flowers come in vivid colours, from creamy-white and chartreuse green to shocking pinks, orange, vermilions and scarlets. Usually, seed is sold in mixtures, but named varieties may also be had from some seedsmen.